Windows Vista® FOR DUMMIES® POCKET EDITION

by Andy Rathbone

WILEY

Wiley Publishing, Inc.

Windows Vista® For Dummies®, Pocket Edition

Published by
Wiley Publishing, Inc.
111 River Street
Hoboken, NJ 07030-5774
www.wiley.com

Published by Wiley Publishing, Inc., Indianapolis, Indiana

Published simultaneously in Canada

For general information on our other products and services, please contact our Customer Care Department within the U.S. at 800-762-2974, outside the U.S. at 317-572-3993, or fax 317-572-4002.

For technical support, please visit www.wiley.com/techsupport.

Wiley also publishes its books in a variety of electronic formats. Some content that appears in print may not be available in electronic books.

ISBN: 978-0-470-41400-2

Manufactured in the United States of America

Contents at a Glance

Publisher's Acknowledgments

We're proud of this book; please send us your comments through our online registration form located at `www.dummies.com/register/`.

Some of the people who helped bring this book to market include the following:

Acquisitions and Editorial

Project Editor:
Jodi Jensen

Executive Editor:
Bob Woerner

Copy Editor:
Jodi Jensen

Editorial Manager:
Jodi Jensen

Composition Services

Project Coordinator:
Kristie Rees

Layout and Graphics:
Reuben W. Davis,
Andrea Hornberger

Proofreaders:
Laura L. Bowman
Amanda Steiner

Publishing and Editorial for Technology Dummies

Richard Swadley, Vice President and Executive Group Publisher

Andy Cummings, Vice President and Publisher

Mary Bednarek, Executive Acquisitions Director

Mary C. Corder, Editorial Director

Publishing for Consumer Dummies

Diane Graves Steele, Vice President and Publisher

Composition Services

Gerry Fahey, Vice President of Production Services

Debbie Stailey, Director of Composition Services

Introduction

Welcome to *Windows Vista For Dummies,* Pocket Edition, an excerpt from the world's best-selling book about Windows Vista! If you're eager to find out about the new stuff Windows Vista has in store for you, plus get some great hands-on computing know how, you've come to the right place.

Why a Book for Dummies?

Well, you're no dummy, that's for sure. But when it comes to Windows and computers, the fascination just isn't there. You want to get your work done, stop, and move on to something more important. You have no intention of changing, and there's nothing wrong with that.

That's where this book comes in handy. Instead of making you a whiz at Windows, it merely dishes out small chunks of useful computing information when you need them. Thumb through this little book to discover just enough about Vista to help you jump in quickly, cleanly, and with minimal stress so that you can move on to all the other important things in your life.

About This Book

Instead of fancy computer jargon, this book covers Windows Vista in plain English. This book is divided into three parts:

- Part I gives you a quick overview of what's new with Vista. If you're wondering what all the hype is about, whether your current computer can run Vista, or which of the five versions of Vista is right for you, Part I is the place to start.
- Part II takes you through the basics of working with Windows Vista: logging on, getting familiar with the Vista desktop, using the Start button, getting to know the taskbar, checking out the new Sidebar, and logging off and shutting down.
- Finally, in Part III, you get to the fun stuff. Here you find out how to play audio CDs and burn music to a CD. You also discover how to play DVD movies on your PC and transfer your digital photos from your camera to your computer.

There's nothing to memorize here. Just turn to the right page, read the brief explanation, and get back to work. Unlike other books, this one enables you to bypass the technical hoopla and still get your work done.

And What about You?

Chances are you already own Windows Vista or are thinking about upgrading. You know what *you* want to do with your computer. The problem lies in making the computer do what you want it to do. You've gotten by one way or another, hopefully with the help of a computer guru — either a friend at the office, somebody down the street, or your fourth-grader.

But when your computer guru isn't around, this book can be a substitute during your times of need. (Keep a doughnut or Pokémon card nearby in case you need a quick bribe.)

Icons Used in This Book

It just takes a glance at Windows Vista to notice its *icons,* which are little push-button pictures for starting various programs. The icons in this book fit right in. They're even a little easier to figure out:

Watch out! This signpost warns you that pointless technical information is coming around the bend. Swerve away from this icon to stay safe from awful technical drivel.

This icon alerts you to juicy information that makes computing easier: A tried-and-true method for keeping the cat from sleeping on top of the monitor, for example.

Don't forget to remember these important points. (Or at least dog-ear the pages so that you can look them up again a few days later.)

The computer won't explode while you're performing the delicate operations associated with this icon. Still, wearing gloves and proceeding with caution is a good idea.

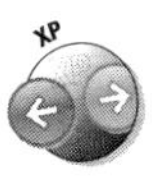

Are you moving to Windows Vista from Windows XP? This icon alerts you to places where Vista works significantly differently from Windows XP.

Part I

What Is Windows Vista?

In This Part

- Getting to know Windows Vista
- Introducing the new features in Vista
- Figuring out whether your PC is powerful enough to run Vista
- Knowing which version of Vista you need

Chances are, you've probably heard about Windows: the boxes and windows and mouse pointer that greet you whenever you turn on your computer. In fact, millions of people all over the world are puzzling over it as you read this book. Most new computers sold today come with a copy of Windows preinstalled — cheerfully greeting you when first turned on.

Part I helps you understand why Windows lives inside your computer and introduces Microsoft's latest Windows version, called *Windows Vista.* It explains how Windows Vista differs from previous Windows versions, whether you should upgrade to Vista, and how well your faithful old PC will weather the upgrade.

Should I Bother Switching to Windows Vista?

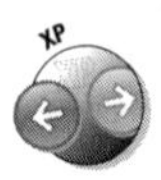

Microsoft releases a new version of Windows every few years. If you bought your PC between 2001 and 2006, you've probably grown accustomed to the mechanics of Windows XP. That leaves the nagging question, why bother upgrading to Windows Vista when Windows XP works just fine?

Actually, if Windows XP is running just fine for you, you probably don't need Windows Vista. But Microsoft hopes the following improvements in Vista will push your hand toward your credit card.

Improved security

Windows Vista's tougher new exterior helps make it more difficult for evil programs to louse up your PC. For example, Vista's built-in Windows Defender program constantly searches your PC for any spyware — small programs that spy on your activities, often showing you pop-up ads and slowing down your PC in the process. Microsoft constantly trains Windows Defender, shown in Figure 1-1, to recognize and squash the newest breeds of spyware.

PCs recognize programs as mere strings of numbers, and they can't tell a good string — a word processor, for example — from a bad string, such as a virus. To solve the identification problem, Vista simply dumps the decision onto *your* shoulders: Whenever a particularly powerful program tries to run on your PC, Vista states, "Windows needs your permission to run this program." Then it leaves you with two choices: Allow or Cancel.

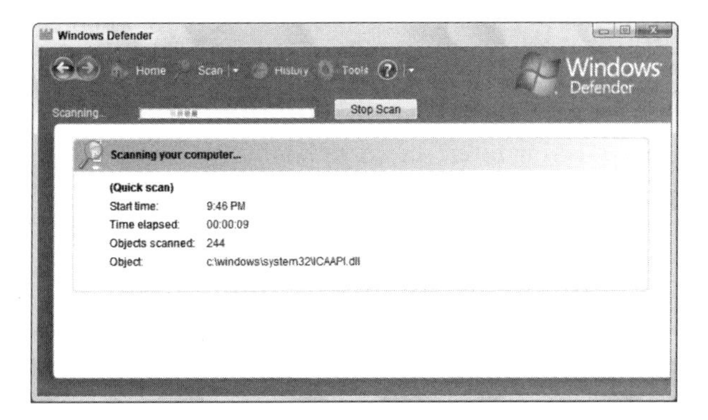

Figure 1-1: Windows Defender is automatically updated by Microsoft to recognize the latest spyware.

Vista doesn't include a free antivirus program. Instead, Microsoft invites you to subscribe to its new Live OneCare antivirus program (`www.windowsonecare.com`) for $49 per year.

New Internet Explorer Version

Vista's new Internet Explorer 7 lets you surf the Web more easily and securely with the following new features:

- **Tabbed browsing:** With Vista, Internet Explorer displays several Web sites simultaneously, each running in a separate page with a clickable tab at the top for easy switching. This tab makes it easier to compare prices from several different shopping sites, for example, or read one Web site while others load in the background. You can even save a group of Web sites as your home page. Then, when you load Internet Explorer, your favorite sites are waiting for you, each in its own tab.

- **Phishing filter:** An evil new industry called *phishing* sends e-mails that pretend to be from finance-related companies, such as banks, PayPal, eBay, and others. The realistic-looking e-mails pretend to alert you to some security problem as they try to trick you into entering your name and precious password. Internet Explorer's new Phishing Filter, shown in Figure 1-2, sniffs out the phishing Web sites before you enter your information.

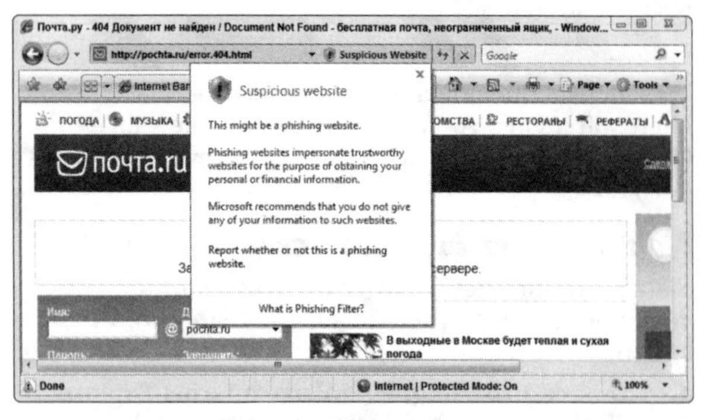

Figure 1-2: The new Phishing Filter alerts you to fake Web sites that try to trick you into entering personal information.

- **Built-in Search box:** The top of Internet Explorer 7 sports a tiny Search box for on-the-fly searches. Although it's programmed to search on Microsoft's own MSN search, you can make it search Google instead. (You find out how to do this and much more in the full version of *Windows Vista For Dummies* from Wiley Publishing.)
- **RSS feeds:** Short for Really Simple Syndication, this feature lets you see headlines from your favorite Web sites in a short drop-down box. RSS feeds also let you know if your favorite sites have any new articles, sparing you a wasted visit. RSS feeds speed up your browsing and, conveniently, leave out the ads.

New Media Player and Media Center

Vista's new version of Media Player sports streamlined, easier-to-use controls. The big star, however, is Vista's Media Center, which not only plays DVDs and music but lets you watch TV on your PC and even record shows onto your hard drive for later viewing.

Recording TV shows requires two important things, however: a TV tuner in your PC and the proper version of Vista. (Vista comes in a startling *five* versions, all described at the end of this part.) Installing a TV tuner can be as simple as plugging a box into your PC's USB port or sliding a card inside your PC. You can find out more about these tasks in *Upgrading and Fixing PCs For Dummies* (published by Wiley Publishing).

DVD burning

Windows Vista lets you copy files and movies to DVDs as well as to CDs without third-party software.

In fact, Vista's updated version of Movie Maker lets you turn your camcorder footage into DVDs that play back on a normal DVD player and TV. Mail them to friends and prepare for a deluge of incoming vacation DVDs, as well.

Calendar

For the first time, Windows now sports a calendar, shown in Figure 1-3, for keeping track of your appointments. You can even publish your calendar to other PCs or Web sites, keeping your appointments synchronized with the calendars of your friends and coworkers.

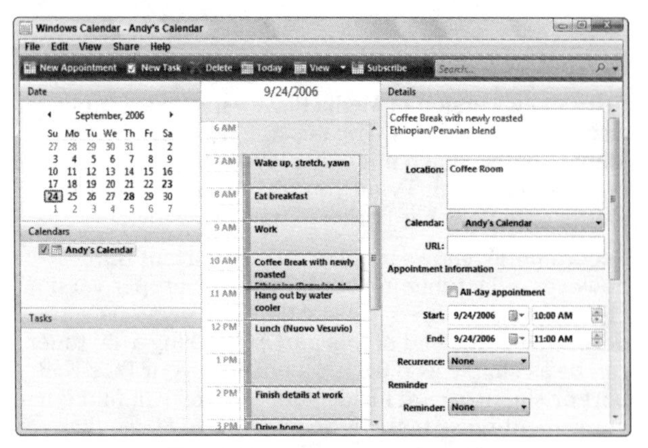

Figure 1-3: Vista's Calendar tracks your appointments and lets you synchronizes your calendar with others.

Easier searching for files

Windows XP really drags its feet when searching for files. Vista, by contrast, spends its idle time fine-tuning an index of every word on your hard drive.

Instead of sending you on a constant search for your files, Vista automatically remembers your files' locations.

Vista looks prettier

Microsoft spent some time decorating Vista with a three-dimensional look (limited to those PCs with powerful graphics capabilities, unfortunately). When you can't find an open window, for example, press the Windows and Tab keys: All the windows appear on your PC in a Flip 3D view, shown in Figure 1-4.

Can My PC Run Vista?

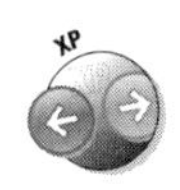

If your PC already runs Windows XP well, it will probably run Vista, but not at its best. Upgrading your PC with a few things can help Vista run better. (For help with this, check out *Upgrading and Fixing PCs For Dummies,* 7th edition, from Wiley Publishing.) Here's the shopping list:

- **Video:** Vista requires powerful graphics for its 3D features, such as Flip 3D (see Figure 1-4). Upgraded video cards can cost more than $100, and they're not available for laptops. If your PC's video lacks the muscle and your wallet lacks the cash, don't despair. Vista simply slips into more casual clothes, letting your PC run without 3D.

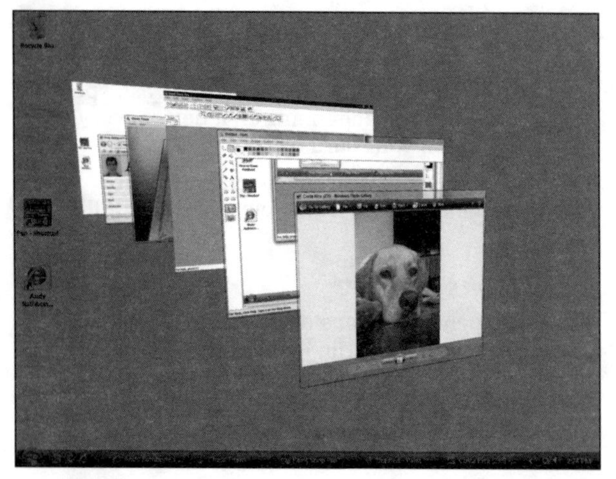

Figure 1-4: The 3D view of your currently open windows. Press Tab or spin your mouse's scroll wheel to flip through the windows.

- **Memory:** For best results, your PC should have 1GB or more of memory. Memory's easy to install and relatively cheap, so don't skimp here.
- **DVD drive:** Unlike Windows XP, which comes on a CD, Windows Vista comes on a *DVD*. That means your PC needs a working DVD drive to install it. That probably won't rule out many PCs these days, but it may rule out some older laptops.

Windows Vista should run most of your current programs without problems. Some, however, won't work, including most security-based programs, such as antivirus and firewall programs. You'll need to contact the program's manufacturer to see whether it'll give you a free upgrade.

Not sure what version of Windows your PC has? Right-click Computer (or My Computer) from the Start menu and choose Properties. That screen states your Windows version.

The Five Flavors of Vista

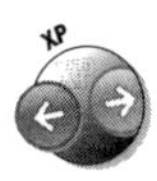

Windows XP came in two easy-to-understand versions: One for home, and one for business. Microsoft confuses things in Vista by splitting it into five different versions, each with a different price tag.

Luckily, only three versions of Vista are aimed at consumers, and most people will probably choose Windows Vista Home Premium. Still, to clear up the confusion, Table 1-1 describes all five versions.

Table 1-1 The Five Flavors of Windows Vista

Version	*What It Does*
Windows Vista Home Basic	Reminiscent of Windows XP Home Edition, this version leaves out Vista's fancier media features, such as DVD burning, HDTV, TV recording, and other similar features.

(continued)

Table 1-1 ***(continued)***

Version	*What It Does*
Windows Vista Home Premium	This version is Windows Vista Home Basic, but with the media features tossed back in. It targets people who watch TV on their PC or who want to create DVDs from their camcorder footage.
Windows Vista Business	Just as with its brethren, Windows XP Professional, this version targets the business market. It includes a fax program, for example, but lacks the media-related features found in Vista Home Premium.
Windows Vista Enterprise	This business market version contains even more tools, such as support for additional languages and larger networks.
Windows Vista Ultimate	A combination of the Home and Business versions, this version targets the wallets of hard-core PC users, such as gamers, people in the video industry, and people who spend their lives in front of their keyboards.

Because Microsoft stuffed all the versions on your Vista DVD, you can upgrade at any time simply by whipping out the credit card and unlocking the features in a different version. Here are some guidelines for home users deciding which version to choose:

- If your PC can't display or record TV shows, and you don't want to make DVDs from your camcorder footage, then save a few bucks by sticking with **Windows Vista Home Basic.** It's fine for word processing, e-mail, and the Internet.
- If you want to burn DVDs and/or record TV shows on your PC, then pony up the cash for **Windows Vista Home Premium.**

Part II

The Desktop, Start Menu, and Other Vista Mysteries

In This Part

- Starting Windows Vista
- Getting to know the desktop and taskbar
- Examining the Sidebar
- Shutting down Windows Vista

This part provides a drive-by tour of Windows Vista. You turn on your computer, start Windows, and spend a few minutes gawking at Vista's neighborhoods: the desktop, the taskbar, the Start menu, and the environmentally correct (and compassionate) Recycle Bin.

The programs you're using hang out on the Windows *desktop* (a fancy word for the Windows background). The taskbar lets you move from one program to another. To invite yet more programs onto the desktop, drop by the Start menu: It's full of push buttons that let you add other programs to the mix.

Welcome to the World of Windows Vista

Starting Windows Vista is as easy as turning on your computer — Windows Vista leaps onto the screen automatically with a futuristic flourish. Vista may throw you a fastball with its first screen: Windows wants you to *log on,* as shown in Figure 2-1, by clicking your name.

Figure 2-1 shows a customized screen. Yours will look different. If you don't see a username listed for you on the Welcome screen, you have three options:

Figure 2-1: Windows Vista wants all users to log on so that it knows who's using the computer at all times.

- **If you just bought the computer, use the account named Administrator.** Designed to give the owner full power over the computer, the Administrator account user can set up new accounts for new users, install programs, burn CDs, start an Internet connection, and access all the files on the computer — even those of other users. Windows Vista needs at least one person to act as administrator, even if your computer isn't connected to other computers. (Get a copy of the full book, *Windows Vista For Dummies,* published by Wiley Publishing, if you care about this stuff.)
- **Use the Guest account.** Designed for household visitors, this account lets guests, such as the babysitter or visiting relatives, use the computer temporarily.
- **No Guest account *and* no username?** Find out who owns the computer and beg that person to set up a username for you.

If you don't want to log on at the Welcome screen, these hidden Welcome screen buttons control other options:

- The little blue button in the screen's bottom-left corner customizes Windows Vista for people with physical challenges in hearing, sight, or manual dexterity. If you push this button by mistake, press Cancel to remove the option menu from your screen without changing any settings.
- To turn off your PC from this sparse opening screen, click the little red button in the screen's bottom-right corner (refer to Figure 2-1). If you

accidentally click it and turn off your PC, don't panic. Press your PC's power button, and your PC returns to this screen.

- Click the little arrow next to the red button in the bottom-right corner, and Vista ends your session by either going to sleep, turning off your PC, or restarting — all explained at the end of this part.

Windows Vista dashes back to this Welcome screen whenever you haven't touched your PC for ten minutes. To stop all this scurrying about, right-click the desktop and choose Personalize. Choose Screen Saver and remove the check mark next to the On Resume, Display Logon Screen option. From now on, you only have to log on when you start up Windows — not throughout the day.

Running Windows Vista for the first time

If you've just installed Windows Vista or you're turning on your computer for the first time, you're treated to a few extra Windows Vista spectacles. The Welcome Center leaves you with the following buttons customized to your particular PC:

- **View Computer Details:** The Welcome Center starts at this page, which lists technical details about your PC: its version of Vista, as well as your PC's processor, memory, video adapter, and so on.
- **Transfer Files and Settings:** Just turned on your *new* Vista PC? This helpful area lets you lug all your old PC's files to your new one (a chore you can walk through in the full book, *Windows Vista For Dummies,* by Wiley Publishing).

- **Add New Users:** Ignore this one unless other people will be sharing your PC. If that's the case, click here to introduce those people to Windows. This area also lets you control what your kids (or roommates) can do on your PC.
- **Connect to the Internet:** Ready to surf and check e-mail? This feature introduces Vista to your Internet connection.
- **Windows Ultimate Extras:** Owners of Vista's Ultimate version find downloadable add-ons here.
- **Windows Anytime Upgrade:** Owners of any other Windows versions can click here to upgrade to a more powerful version.
- **What's New in Windows Vista:** Handy for Windows XP upgraders, this button introduces you to the new features in your particular version of Vista.
- **Personalize Windows:** Head here to splash a new screen across your desktop, change Vista's colors, or tweak your monitor.
- **Register Windows Online:** Head here to, uh, sign up for Microsoft's e-mail marketing blurbs.
- **Windows Media Center:** This button begins the process of revving up Windows Media Center to record TV shows.
- **Windows Basics:** Designed for owners of their first PC, this tutorial explains how to use the mouse and keyboard, as well as files and folders.
- **Ease of Access Center:** People with physical challenges will enjoy Vista's variety of accessibility tools here.

(continued)

(continued)

- **Back Up and Restore Center:** Find out all about this feature in the full version of *Windows Vista For Dummies* (Wiley Publishing).
- **Windows Vista Demos:** Little movies in Vista's Help program help you with different Vista tasks.
- **Control Panel:** The nerve center of your PC, the Control Panel lets you tweak how Vista interacts with your PC.

Vista initially shows only a few buttons, but to see them all, click Show All 14 Items along the bottom of the Welcome Center.

To see more information about any of these tasks, click the button once. Or double-click a button to move directly to that particular chore. To make the Welcome Center stop welcoming you every time you turn on your PC, remove the check mark from the Run at Startup box.

Navigating the Desktop

Normally, people want their desktops to be horizontal, not vertical. Keeping pencils from rolling off a normal desk is hard enough. But in Windows Vista, your monitor's screen is known as the Windows *desktop,* and that's where all your work takes place. You can create files and folders right on your new electronic desktop and arrange them all across the screen. Each program runs in its own little *window* on top of the desktop.

Windows Vista starts with a freshly scrubbed, empty desktop. After you've been working for a while, your desktop will fill up with *icons* — little push buttons that load your files with a quick double-click of the mouse. Some people leave their desktops strewn with icons for easy access. Others organize their work: When they finish working on something, they store it in a *folder.*

The desktop boasts four main parts, as shown in Figure 2-2.

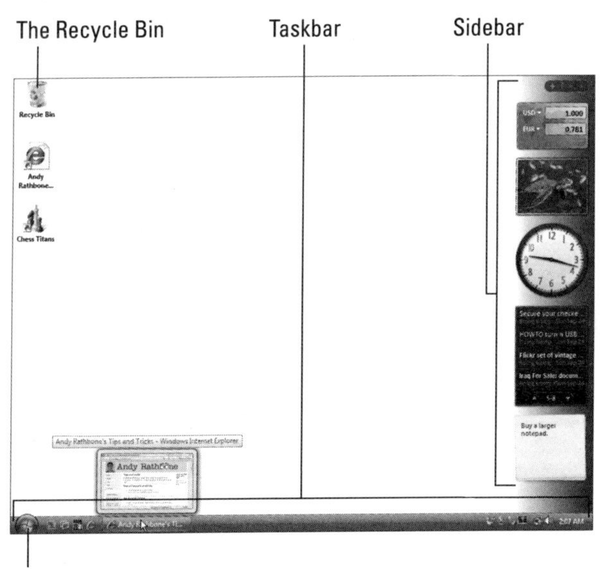

Figure 2-2: The Windows Vista desktop, which spreads across your entire computer screen, has four main parts.

The following list describes the four parts of the desktop:

- **Taskbar:** Resting lazily along the desktop's bottom edge, the taskbar lists the programs and files you're currently working on. (Point at any program's name on the taskbar to see a name or thumbnail photo of that program.)
- **Start menu:** Seen at the taskbar's left edge, the Start menu works like a waiter: It presents menus at your bidding, letting you choose what program to run.
- **Sidebar:** Windows Vista's desktop newcomer, the *Sidebar,* clings along the right edge, offering a plethora of customized gadgets such as weather forecasters, search boxes, and Sudoku games.
- **Recycle Bin:** The desktop's *Recycle Bin,* that little wastebasket-shaped icon, stores your recently deleted files for easy retrieval.

Here are a few key points about the desktop:

- You can start new projects directly from your desktop: Right-click the desktop, choose New, and select a project from the pop-up menu, be it adding a new Contact or loading a favorite program.

Are you befuddled about some object's reason for being? Rest the pointer over the mysterious doodad, and Windows pops up a little box explaining what that thing is or does. Right-click the object, and Windows Vista usually tosses up a menu listing nearly everything you can do with it.

- All the icons on your desktop may suddenly disappear, leaving it completely empty. Chances are Windows Vista hid them in a misguided attempt to be helpful. To bring your work back to life, right-click your empty desktop and choose View from the pop-up menu. Finally, make sure the Show Desktop Icons box has a check mark so that everything stays visible.

Jazzing up Your Desktop's Background

To jazz up your desktop, Windows Vista covers it with pretty pictures known as a *background.* (Most people refer to the background as *wallpaper.*)

When you tire of the Vista's normal scenic garb, choose your own picture — any picture stored on your computer. Here's how:

1. **Right-click on a blank part of the desktop, choose Personalize, and click Desktop Background.**
2. **Click any of the available pictures (see Figure 2-3), and Vista quickly places it onto your desktop's background.**
3. **Click the Save button if you find one you want to keep on your desktop.**

   Click the Picture Location menu to see more pictures; if you're still searching, move to the next step.
4. **(Optional) Click the Browse button and click a file from inside your Pictures folder.**

   This assumes, of course, that your personal digital photos are stored in the Pictures folder.

Figure 2-3: Try out different backgrounds.

5. **When you find the picture you want, exit the program. Your chosen photo stays stuck to your desktop as the background.**

Here are some more tips for sprucing up your desktop:

- As you browse through different pictures, Windows Vista automatically decides whether the image should be *tiled* repeatedly across the screen, *centered* directly in the middle, or *stretched* to fill the entire screen. To override

Windows' automatic choice, select your own preference from the How Should the Picture Be Positioned? area along the bottom of the window. Feel free to experiment to see each effect.

- You can easily borrow any picture on the Internet for a background. Right-click the Web site's picture and select Set as Background from the pop-up menu. Microsoft sneakily copies the image onto your desktop as its new background. (You can also right-click any photo in your Pictures folder and choose Set as Background — handy for quick background changes.)
- To change Windows Vista's entire *look,* right-click the desktop, choose Personalize, and choose Theme. Aimed at heavy-duty procrastinators, different themes splash different colors across Windows' various buttons, borders, and boxes. (If you download any Themes offered on the Internet, check them with antivirus software.)

The Start Button's Reason to Live

The bright-blue Start button lives in the bottom-left corner of the desktop, where it's always ready for action. By clicking the Start button, you can start programs, adjust Windows Vista's settings, find help for sticky situations, or shut down Windows Vista and get away from the computer for a while.

Click the Start button once, and the first layer of menus pops out, as shown in Figure 2-4.

Your Documents, Pictures, and Music folders are always one click away on the Start menu. These folders are specially designed for their contents. The Pictures folder, for example, displays little thumbnails of your digital photos. So what's the biggest perk to these three folders? Keeping your files in these folders helps you remember where you stored them.

- Windows thoughtfully places your most frequently used programs along the left side of the Start menu for easy point 'n' click action.
- See the words *All Programs* near the Start menu's bottom left? Click there, and yet another menu opens to offer more options. (That new menu covers up the first, though; to bring back the first, click the word Back.)
- Strangely enough, you also click the Start button when you want to *stop* using Windows. (You click one of the Off buttons in the bottom right of the Start menu.)

Figure 2-4: The Start button in Windows Vista hides dozens of menus for starting programs.

The Start menu's prime real estate

When the Start menu pops up (refer to Figure 2-4), it always shows you the items offered in the following list. You use these items constantly in Windows:

Internet Explorer: This option lets you visit the Internet.

E-mail: Choose this command to send or receive e-mail with Vista's new Windows Mail program.

Recently Used Programs: The Start menu's left side constantly updates to list the icons for your most frequently used programs for quick launches.

Search box: Conveniently placed directly above the Start button, this area lets you find files by typing a bit of their contents — a few words in an e-mail, a document, a band name, a program's name, or anything else. Press Enter, and Vista quickly dredges up the file for you.

Username: The name of your user account appears at the Start menu's top-right corner. Click here to see a folder containing all your files, as well as your Documents, Pictures, and Music folders.

Documents: This command quickly opens your Documents folder, making it more imperative than ever to always store your work here.

Pictures: Keep your digital pictures in this folder. Each picture's icon is a tiny thumbnail image of your photo.

Music: Store your digital music in here so that Media Player can find and play it more easily.

Games: Windows Vista offers several new games, including a decent chess game.

Search: The word Search on the Start menu lets you search for files in precise terms — say, all files created in the last two months containing the word *oyster*. Use the Search box along the bottom of the Start menu when making more general searches.

Recent Items: If you've viewed a file within the past few hours, chances are it appears here for quick access.

Computer: This option displays your computer's storage areas: folders, disk drives, CD drives, digital cameras, and other attached goodies.

Network: If your computer connects with other computers through a network, click here to visit them.

Connect To: This area lets you connect to different networks. It's a quick way for those using a laptop to connect to a wireless network, as well as a one-click Internet entrance for people with dialup Internet connections.

Control Panel: This area lets you adjust your computer's oodles of confusing settings.

Default programs: Click here to control which program steps in when you open a file. Here's where you tell Windows to let iTunes handle your music rather than, say, Media Player.

Help and Support: Befuddled? Click here for an answer.

Sleep/Power: Clicking here either puts your PC to sleep or turns it off, as explained in this part's last section.

Lock: This command locks your user account, letting other people log on without accessing your files.

Customizing the Start menu

The Windows Vista Start menu works great — until you're hankering for something that's not listed on the menu or something you rarely use is getting in the way. Here are a couple ways you can make the Start menu your own:

- **Add a favorite program's icon to the Start button menu:** Right-click the program's icon and choose Pin to Start Menu from the pop-up menu. Windows copies that icon to your Start menu's left column. (From there, you may drag it to the All Programs area, if you want.)
- **Purge unwanted icons from the Start menu's left column:** Right-click the icon and choose either Unpin from Start Menu or Remove from This List. Removing an icon from the Start menu doesn't remove the actual program from your computer; it just removes one of many push buttons that launches it.

When you install a program, the program almost always adds itself to the Start menu *automatically.* Then the program boldly announces its presence by displaying its name with a different background color.

Making Windows start programs automatically

Many people sit down at a computer, turn it on, and go through the same mechanical process of loading their oft-used programs. Believe it or not, Windows Vista can automate this task. The solution is the Startup folder, found lurking in the Start button's All Programs menu. When Windows Vista wakes up, it peeks inside that Startup folder. If it finds a program lurking inside, it immediately tosses that program onto the screen.

To make your favorite programs wake up along with Windows Vista, follow these steps:

1. **Click the Start button and choose All Programs.**
2. **Right-click the Start menu's Startup icon and choose Open.**

   The Startup icon, which lives in the Start menu's All Programs area, opens as a folder.
3. **Drag and drop any of your favorite programs or files into the Startup folder.**

   Windows Vista automatically places shortcuts to those programs inside the Startup folder.
4. **Close the Startup folder.**

   Now, whenever you turn on your PC and log onto your user account, Vista automatically loads those programs or files so they'll be waiting for you.

Bellying Up to the Taskbar

This section introduces one of Windows Vista's handiest tricks, so pull your chair in a little closer. Whenever you run more than one window on the desktop, there's a big problem: Programs and windows tend to overlap, making them difficult to locate.

Windows Vista's solution is the *taskbar* — a special area that keeps track of all your open programs. Shown in Figure 2-5, the taskbar normally lives along the bottom of your screen, although you can move it to any edge you want. (***Hint:*** Just drag it from edge to edge. If it doesn't move, right-click the taskbar and click Lock the Taskbar to remove the check mark by its name.)

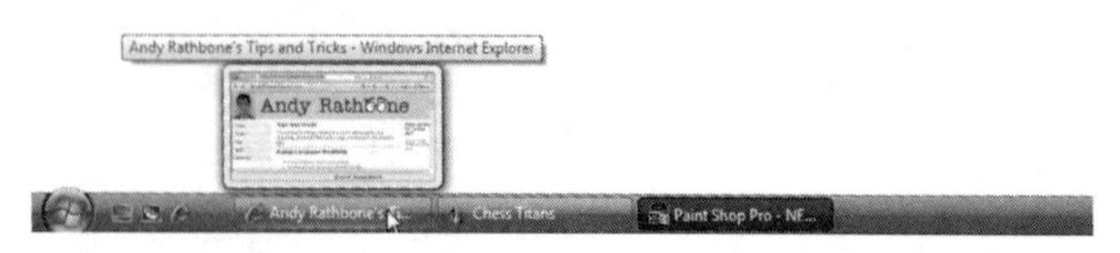

Figure 2-5: Click buttons for currently running programs on the taskbar.

See how the button for Paint Shop Pro looks darker than the other taskbar buttons in Figure 2-5? That's because Paint Shop Pro is currently the *active* window on the desktop: It's the program waiting for you to start working. One of your taskbar's buttons always looks darker unless you close or minimize all the windows on your desktop.

From the taskbar, you can perform powerful magic on your open windows, as described in the following list:

- To work with a program listed on the taskbar, click its name. The window rises to the surface and rests atop any other open windows.
- To close a window listed on the taskbar, *right-click* its name and choose Close from the pop-up menu. The program quits, just as if you'd chosen its Exit command from within its own window. (The departing program gives you a chance to save your work before it quits and walks off the screen.)
- If the taskbar keeps hiding below the screen's bottom edge, point the mouse at the screen's bottom edge until the taskbar surfaces. Then right-click the taskbar, choose Properties, and remove the check mark from the Auto-hide the Taskbar check box.

Clicking the taskbar's sensitive areas

Like a crafty card player, the taskbar comes with a few tips and tricks. For example, here's the lowdown on the icons near the taskbar's right edge, shown in Figure 2-6, known as the *notification area.*

Figure 2-6: These taskbar icons help with specific tasks.

- **Clock:** Hold the mouse pointer over the clock, and Windows Vista shows the current day and date. Click the clock to see a handy monthly calendar. If you want to change the time, date, or add a second time zone, click the clock and choose Change Date and Time Settings.

- **Speaker:** Click the little speaker icon to adjust the sound card's volume.
- **Arrow:** Sometimes the taskbar hides things. Click the little arrow on the far left, and a few hidden icons may slide out. (Check out the next section, "Customizing the taskbar," for tips and tricks affecting these icons.)
- **Other icons:** These often appear next to the clock, depending on what Windows Vista is up to. When you print, for example, a little printer icon appears. Laptops often show a battery-power-level gauge, and a network icon shows when you're connected to the Internet. As with all the other icons down there, if you double-click the printer or battery gauge, Windows Vista brings up information about the printer's or battery's status.
- **Blank part:** The empty portions of the taskbar also hide a menu. Want to minimize all your desktop's open windows in a hurry? Right-click on a blank part of the taskbar and choose Show the Desktop from the pop-up menu.

To organize your open windows, right-click a blank part of the taskbar and choose one of the tile commands. Windows Vista scoops up all your open windows and lays them back down in neat, orderly squares.

Customizing the taskbar

Windows Vista brings a whirlwind of options for the lowly taskbar. Right-click the Start button, choose Properties, and click the Taskbar tab. Table 2-1 explains the options, as well as some recommendations for them. (You need to remove the check mark by Lock the Taskbar before some of these options will work.)

Table 2-1 Customizing the Taskbar

Setting	***Recommendations***
Lock the Taskbar	Clicking here makes Windows Vista lock the taskbar in place, keeping you from changing its appearance. You can't drag it upward to make it larger, for example. Lock it, but only after the taskbar is set up the way you like.
Auto-Hide the Taskbar	Selecting this option makes the taskbar *automatically* hide itself when you're not near it. (Point at the bottom edge of the screen to bring the taskbar back up.) I leave this option unchecked to keep the taskbar always in view.
Keep the Taskbar on Top of Other Windows	This option keeps the taskbar always visible, covering up any windows that may be low on the screen. I leave this checked.
Group Similar Taskbar Buttons	When you open lots of windows and programs, Windows accommodates the crowd by grouping similar windows under one button: All open documents in Microsoft Word stack on one Microsoft Word button, for example. This option protects the taskbar from overcrowding, so keep it checked.
Show Quick Launch	This setting shows your Quick Launch toolbar, that collection of handy icons hanging out by your Start button. (I cover it and other toolbars later in this part.)

(continued)

Table 2-1 *(continued)*

Setting	*Recommendations*
Show Windows Previews (Thumbnails)	This option tells the taskbar to show a thumbnail photo of a program when you hover your mouse pointer over the program's taskbar button. Leave this option selected to make it easier to locate misplaced windows. (This option is unavailable unless your PC packs powerful graphics.)

Feel free to experiment with the taskbar until it looks right for you. It won't break. After you set it up just the way you want, select the Lock the Taskbar check box described in Table 2-1.

The taskbar's crazy toolbars

Your taskbar won't always be a steadfast, unchanging friend. Microsoft lets you customize it even further, often beyond the point of recognition.

To turn a toolbar on or off, right-click on a blank part of the taskbar (even the clock will do) and choose Toolbars from the pop-up menu. A menu leaps out, offering the toolbars described in the following list:

- **Address:** Choose this toolbar, and part of your taskbar becomes a place for typing Web sites to visit. It's convenient, but so is Internet Explorer, which does the same thing.

- **Windows Media Player:** When turned on, the toolbar shown in Figure 2-7 turns into a handy button panel for controlling your minimized Windows Media Player.

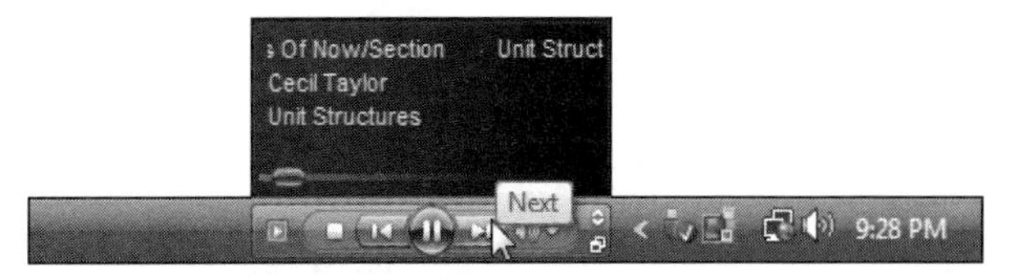

Figure 2-7: The Windows Media Player toolbar.

- **Links:** This toolbar adds quick access to your favorite Web sites. Click it to visit any Web site listed in Internet Explorer's Favorites menu.
- **Desktop:** Techies who find the Start menu burdensome add this toolbar for quick access to all their PC's resources. It lets you browse through files, network locations, and Control Panel menus by snaking your way through all the menus.
- **Quick Launch:** The only toolbar Vista displays when first installed, this places a handful of handy icons, as shown earlier in Figure 2-5, next to your Start button. (Add your own icons to this toolbar by dragging and dropping them.)

- **New Toolbar:** Click here to choose *any* folder to add as a toolbar. For example, you can choose your Documents folder for quick browsable access to all its files and folders.

Toolbars fall into the love 'em or hate 'em category. And some toolbars, like the Tablet PC Input Panel, only work when you attach an expensive, touch-sensitive pad to your PC. Feel free to experiment until you decide which camp you fall into.

Toolbars are *supposed* to be dragged around with the mouse. When the taskbar is unlocked, grab the toolbar by its *handle,* a vertical line by the toolbar's name. Drag the handle to the left or right to change a toolbar's size.

The Sidebar

If your Sidebar doesn't grace your desktop, fire it up: Right-click the little icon (shown in the margin) in the taskbar's notification area — that icon-packed area next to the desktop's clock — and choose Show Sidebar. The Sidebar springs to life, as shown in Figure 2-8.

Figure 2-8: The Sidebar displays *Gadgets*.

To see Windows Vista's collection of built-in *Gadgets* (minuscule programs that snap on and off their panel), click the little plus sign near the top of the Sidebar. A window pops up offering a calendar and stock ticker, among others. Click Get More Gadgets Online to visit Gadget nirvana: A Web site packed with Gadgets, ready for the picking.

- Prefer your Sudoku game gadget on top? Drag it up there. You can even drag Gadgets off the Sidebar and onto the desktop — if you have a huge enough monitor to sacrifice the space.
- To change a Gadget's settings — choose which photos appear in your slide show, for example — point at the Gadget and click the tiny wrench icon that appears. To remove a Gadget completely, click the little X, instead.

Logging Off Windows

You stop using Windows Vista the same way you start: by using the Start button, that friendly little helper you've been using all along. (If the Start menu is hiding, hold down Ctrl and press Esc to bring it back.) You want to use one of the two buttons resting at the bottom of the Start menu:

Sleep/Power: Sleep mode (top icon in the margin) comes in handy when you won't be using your PC for several hours but want to start up where you left off. Designed for impatient desktop users, this option memorizes your currently open windows, and then turns off your PC. When you turn on your PC, your open programs and documents appear on the desktop where you left them. On laptops, this option is a Power button (bottom icon in the margin) that simply turns off your PC.

Lock: Meant for short trips to the water cooler, this option locks your PC and places your user account picture on the screen. When you return, type your password, and Vista instantly displays your desktop, just as you left it. This option appears on both laptops and desktop PCs.

Windows Vista offers several other ways to close your session. Look closely at the arrow to the right of the Lock button. Click the arrow to see up to seven options:

- **Switch User:** If somebody else just wants to borrow the computer for a few minutes, choose Switch User. The Welcome screen appears, but Windows keeps your open programs waiting in the background. When you switch back, everything's just as you left it.
- **Log Off:** Choose this option when you're through working at the PC and somebody else wants a go at it. Windows saves your work and your settings and returns to the Welcome screen, ready for the next user.
- **Lock:** For some reason, Microsoft offers the Lock option again (described earlier in this section).
- **Restart:** Only choose this option when Windows Vista screws something up: for example, several

programs crash, or Windows seems to be acting awfully weird. Windows Vista turns off and reloads itself, hopefully feeling refreshed.

- **Sleep:** New to Vista, this option saves a copy of your work in your PC's memory *and* on its hard drive and then slumbers into a low-power state. When you turn your PC back on, Vista presents your desktop, programs, and windows as if you'd never left. (On a laptop, Sleep saves your work only to memory. Should the battery life grow threateningly low, Sleep dumps it onto the hard drive and turns off your laptop.)
- **Hibernate:** Found on some laptops, this option copies your work to your hard drive and then turns off your PC — a process requiring more battery power than Sleep mode.
- **Shut Down:** Choose this option when nobody else will be using the computer until the next morning. Windows Vista saves everything and turns off your computer.

When you tell Windows Vista that you want to quit, it searches through all your open windows to see whether you've saved all your work. If it finds any work you've forgotten to save, it lets you know so that you can click the OK button to save it. Whew!

Don't just press your PC's Off button to turn off your PC. Instead, be sure to shut down Windows Vista through one of its official Off options: Sleep, Hibernate, or Shut Down. Otherwise, Windows Vista can't properly prepare your computer for the dramatic event, leading to future troubles.

Part III

Having Fun with Music, Movies, and Photos

In This Part

- Playing CDs and DVDs
- Copying CDs to your hard drive
- Making a music CD
- Copying digital photos to your computer

Windows Vista comes with Media Player 11, which lets you play CDs and DVDs, copy music to your PC, and burn your music to a CD.

In addition to Media Player, Windows Vista also comes loaded with some great software that lets you manage photos from your digital camera. The following sections help you have some fun with your CDs, DVDs, and photos.

Playing CDs

To play a CD, you open Windows Media Player from the Start menu's All Programs area. As long as you insert the CD in the CD drive correctly (usually label-side up), playing a music CD is one of Media Player's easiest tasks. The biggest stumbling block comes with the pop-up dialog box, shown in Figure 3-1, that appears when you insert the CD.

Eager to please, Windows Vista begs to know how to handle your newly inserted CD. Should it *play* the CD with Media Player? *Rip* (copy) its music onto your hard drive? Play it in *Media Center* — another Vista program? *Open it* in Computer and display its files and folders?

Here's the big problem with the dialog box: The fine print reads, "Always do this for audio CDs." No matter what option you choose, if you have this check box selected, Vista automatically makes that choice the next time you insert a CD.

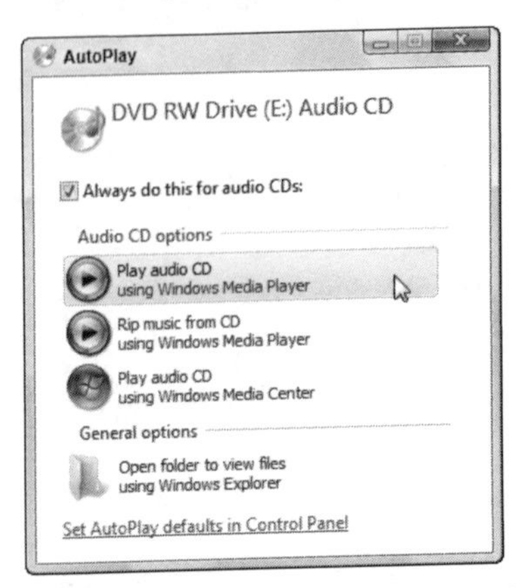

Figure 3-1: When you insert a CD, Windows Vista asks you what to do with it.

To keep Vista from always taking a particular action, click to remove the check mark from that box. *Then* make your choice.

If you're not interested in anything but playing CDs, however, leave the box checked and choose Play Audio CD using Windows Media Player. Then Vista automatically plays any music CD you insert into your PC's drive. Here are a couple of tips about playing CDs:

- Too flustered for quick decisions? Pressing the Esc key kicks the dialog box off your screen until the next time you insert a CD.
- When inserting a music CD, don't choose the Open Folder to View Files option. That brings up a pointless list of numbered files named Track. Windows Vista won't let you copy songs to your PC that way; you must click Media Player's Rip button, instead.

If Vista mistakenly displays the CD's files instead of playing the darn thing, choose Default Programs from the Start menu. Choose Change AutoPlay Settings and change the Audio CD drop-down menu to Play Audio CD Using Windows Media Player. Or, to see the dialog box shown in Figure 3-1 whenever you insert a CD, choose Ask Me Every Time from this drop-down menu.

Press F7 to mute Media Player's sound.

Playing DVDs

Media Player plays DVDs as well as CDs, letting your laptop do double-duty as a portable DVD player. Grab your favorite DVD, some headphones, and watch what *you* like during that next long flight.

Although Media Player plays, burns, and copies CDs, it can't copy a DVD's movie to your hard drive, nor can it duplicate a movie DVD. (Remember that black FBI notice at the beginning of each DVD warning you that copies are illegal?)

When you insert a DVD into your DVD drive, Media Player presents a dialog box, much like Figure 3-1 shown in the previous section, asking what it should do with it. To avoid that distraction, select the Always Do This for DVD Movies check box and then click Play DVD Video using Windows Media Player. Media Player will play the DVD immediately, usually pausing at the opening screen.

Media Player works very much like your TV's DVD player, with the mouse acting as the remote. Click the on-screen words or buttons to make the DVD do your bidding.

Copying CDs to Your PC

Unlike older versions of Media Player, Vista's Media Player can create MP3s, the industry standard for digital music. But until you tell the player that you want MP3 files, it creates *WMA* files that won't play on many portable players.

To make Media Player create songs with the more versatile MP3 format instead of WMA, press Alt to reveal the menu, choose Tools, choose Options, and click the Rip Music tab. Choose MP3 instead of WMA from the Format pull-down menu and nudge the audio quality over a tad from 128 to 192, or even 256, for better sound.

To copy a CD to your PC's hard drive, follow these steps:

1. **Open Media Player, insert a music CD, and click the Rip button.**

   You may need to push a button on the front of the drive before the tray ejects. Media Player connects to the Internet, identifies your CD, and fills in the album's name, artist, and song titles. Then the program begins copying the CD's songs to your PC and listing their titles in the Library. You're through.

   If Media Player can't find the songs' titles automatically, move ahead to Step 2.

2. **Click Find Album Info, if necessary.**

   If Media Player comes up empty-handed — a common occurrence when you're not connected to the Internet — fill in the titles yourself. Right-click the first track and choose Find Album Info. Then choose Enter Information for a CD That You Burned. Finally, fill in Media Player's form with the artist and song title information.

Burning Music CDs

What if you want to duplicate a CD, perhaps to create a disposable copy of your favorite CD to play in your car? No sense scratching up your original. Unfortunately, neither Media Player nor Windows Vista offers a Duplicate CD option. Instead, you must jump through the following five hoops to create a new CD with the same songs as the original CD:

1. **Rip (copy) the music to your hard drive.**
2. **Insert a blank CD into your writable CD drive.**
3. **Click the Library button and choose Album to see your saved CDs.**
4. **Right-click the album in your library and choose Add to Burn List.**

   Or, right-click the playlist containing the music you want to burn to the CD and choose Add to Burn List.
5. **Click the Start Burn button.**

Now, for the fine print. Media Player compresses your songs as it saves them on your hard drive, throwing out some audio quality in the process. Burning them back to CD won't replace that lost quality. If you want *true* duplicates of your CDs, buy CD-burning software from your local office supply or computer store.

Moving Photos from Your Camera to Your Computer

Most digital cameras come with software that grabs your camera's photos and places them into your computer. But you needn't install it, nor even bother trying to figure it out. Windows Vista's built-in software easily fetches photos from nearly any make and model of digital camera when you follow these steps:

1. **Plug the camera's cable into your computer.**

   Most cameras come with two cables: One that plugs into your TV set for viewing, and another that plugs into your PC. You need to find the one that plugs into your PC for transferring photos.

   Plug the transfer cable's small end into your camera, and the larger end into your computer's *USB port,* a rectangular-looking hole about one-half-inch long and one-quarter-inch high. (Most USB ports live on the back of the computer, but newer computers offer them closer to the front.)

2. **Turn on your camera, if it's not already turned on, and wait for Windows Vista to recognize it.**

   If you're plugging in the camera for the first time, Windows Vista sometimes heralds the camera's presence with a small pop-up window above your taskbar by the clock.

If Windows Vista doesn't recognize your camera, make sure that the camera is set to Display mode — which lets you see the photos on its screen — rather than Shoot mode, which you use to take pictures. Also, try unplugging the cable from your PC, waiting a few seconds, and then plugging it back in.

3. **When the AutoPlay window appears, click Import Pictures Using Windows.**

   When you first plug a digital camera into a PC running Vista, the AutoPlay window (shown in Figure 3-2) appears. Make sure that a check mark appears in the Always Do This for This Device check box and click Import Pictures Using Windows. This tells Vista to automatically grab your camera's pictures whenever you connect the camera to your PC.

   Don't see the AutoPlay window? Try opening Computer from the Start menu and double-clicking your camera icon.

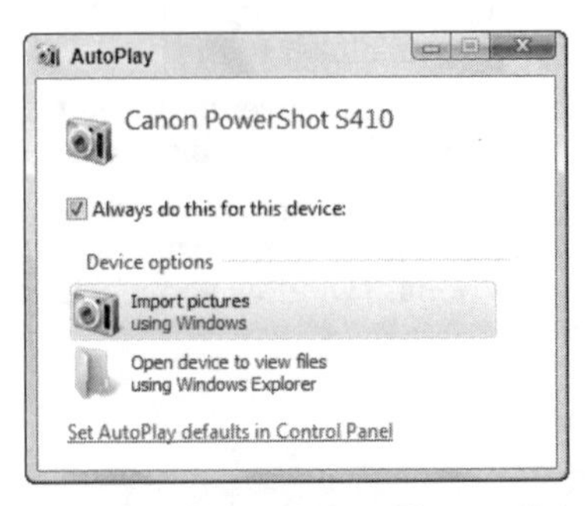

Figure 3-2: Choose Import Pictures Using Windows so that Vista automatically extracts your camera's photos.

4. **Type a *tag* or name for your photos and click Import.**

   Type a descriptive word or two to describe the photos, as shown in Figure 3-3. Type the word **Cat**, for example, and Windows Vista names the incoming photos as Cat 001, Cat 002, Cat 003, and so on. Later, you can find these pictures by searching for the word **Cat**.

   Click Import to bring your camera's photos into your PC and automatically name them.

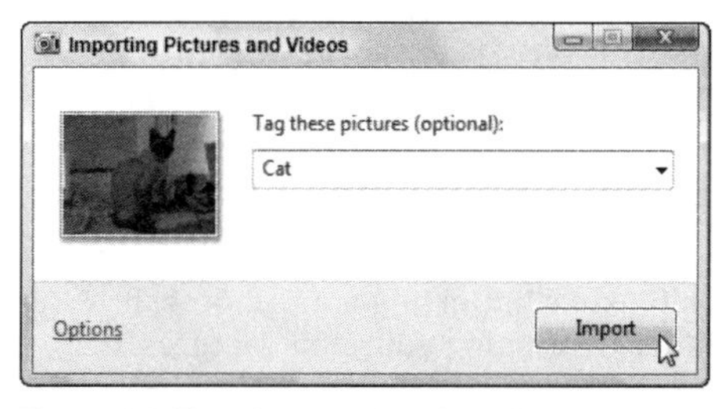

Figure 3-3: Type in a tag that describes your photos.

Clicking the word Options, shown in the lower-left corner in Figure 3-3, lets you change how Vista imports your photos. It's worth a look-see, as it lets you undo any options you may have mistakenly chosen when first importing your photos.

5. **Click Erase After Importing.**

   If you don't delete your camera's photos after importing them into your PC, you won't have room to take more photos. Click Erase After

Importing in the Importing Pictures and Videos dialog box, and Vista erases the camera's photos, saving you the trouble of rummaging through your camera's menus.

6. **If asked, let Windows correct your picture's rotation.**

   When Windows notices that you've turned your camera sideways to take a picture — which usually happens when you take photos of trees or small groups of standing people — take it up on its offer to rotate your photos by clicking Yes. That keeps your photos from showing up sideways on your monitor.

   Some older cameras don't tell Windows when you've turned the camera sideways for a photo, so you may not see this option.

When Windows finishes importing your photos, it displays the folder containing your new pictures.